Numbers

To Parents

This book is designed for children from the age of 2 upwards to help them to learn about the numbers 0 to 9. There are three aspects of number that young children need to come to understand: numbers used as **sets** to answer the question 'How many?' — for example, I have three sisters, four cups etc; numbers used as a way of **placing things in an order** — first, second, third etc; and, lastly, numbers used as **names** — the number five bus, etc. This book helps develop the first concept — numbers used to count sets or groups of things. It starts at 0, to introduce the important concept of zero, and then on each page asks the child to find a set of animals. It also helps the child to learn the names of each number up to 9. Here are some ways you may like to use this book with your child:

1. Reading to your child: always allow plenty of time for the child to look at and talk about the pictures.

2. Ask your child to find the answer to the question 'Who are we?' by looking carefully at each picture. Point out the details mentioned in the text, for example, the three little eggs belonging to the three birds. At the age of 2 your child will probably only be ready to cope with the concept of one and more than one. But it will be valuable to him or her to hear you counting the animals.

   By the age of 4 he or she may be able to count them with you. Don't worry if your child finds this difficult — counting each object is a skill that can take a long time to develop. It involves much more than being able to recite the numbers one to ten in order.

3. There are several other examples of the number on each page — such as five butterflies on the five page, nine trees on the nine page. On further readings of the book see if your child can count out some of these too.

4. Try to find examples of numbers at home and when you're out together. You could play a counting game by asking your child to collect two shoes, three pencils etc. Help your child with the names of the numbers — you could concentrate on a particular number on a particular day.

5. Above all, ensure you both have fun with the book! Give plenty of praise and don't allow the counting to become a chore — there will be plenty of time for your child to develop these early number skills during the first year at school.

Numbers

Written and designed by
David Bennett

Illustrated by
Dom Mansell

o

This is the cage where
I sang each day.
The door was left open
So I flew away.

Who am I?

There is **1** of me.

I've got one trunk,
It's so full of power,
It sucks up the water
And gives me a shower.

Who am I?

There are **2** of us.

We each have two eyes
That are big, black and round.
We play in the trees,
High up from the ground.

Who are we?

There are **3** of us.

We each have a nest,
With three little eggs
And when we sit down,
You can't see our legs.

Who are we?

There are **4** of us.

We each have four legs
That go clippety-clop.
We can run, we can jump,
But we really can't hop.

Who are we?

There are 5 of us.

On each of our feet,
We have five wriggly toes.
We are covered in fur —
We don't need to wear clothes!

Who are we?

There are **6** of us.

We have six little legs
To cling to the flowers.
We go buzz, buzz, buzz,
In the garden for hours.

Who are we?

There are **7** of us.

On our pretty red wings
There are seven black spots.
We crawl around plants,
And hide in flower pots.

Who are we?

There are **8** of us.

We have eight spindly legs
For scuttling around.
People scream when they see us —
We don't make a sound.

Who are we?

There are 9 of us.

We have nine babies each,
All hopping around.
We play in the fields,
But sleep underground.

Who are we?